Animals from Head to Tail

DOGS FROM HEAD TO TAIL

By Cole Mair

Gareth Stevens Publishing

Please visit our website, www.garethstevens.com. For a free color catalog of all our high-quality books, call toll free 1-800-542-2595 or fax 1-877-542-2596.

Cataloging-in-Publication Data

Names: Mair, Cole.
Title: Dogs from head to tail / Cole Mair.
Description: New York : Gareth Stevens Publishing, 2017. | Series: Animals from head to tail | Includes index.
Identifiers: ISBN 9781482445435 (pbk.) | ISBN 9781482445374 (library bound) | ISBN 9781482445251 (6 pack)
Subjects: LCSH: Dogs–Juvenile literature. | Dogs–Physiology–Juvenile literature.
Classification: LCC SF426.5 M35 2017 | DDC 636.7–dc23

First Edition

Published in 2017 by
Gareth Stevens Publishing
111 East 14th Street, Suite 349
New York, NY 10003

Editor: Ryan Nagelhout
Designer: Katelyn E. Reynolds

Photo credits: Cover, pp. 1, 5 (dalmatian spots), 11, 17, 24 (bulldog) Rita Kochmarjova/Shutterstock.com; pp. 5 (ears), 7 Drew Horne/Shutterstock.com; pp. 5 (nose), 9 Vaobullan/Shutterstock.com; pp. 5 (great dane legs), 13 Dmussman/Shutterstock.com; pp. 5 (tail), 23 Russ Beinder/Shutterstock.com; p. 15 siloto/Shutterstock.com; pp. 19, 24 (boxer) vdovin_vn/Shutterstock.com; p. 21 InBetweentheBlinks/Shutterstock.com.

Printed in the United States of America

CPSIA compliance information: Batch #CS16GS: For further information contact Gareth Stevens, New York, New York at 1-800-542-2595.

Contents

Dogs are great
from head to tail!

Many dogs
have big ears.

Dogs have a great sense of smell.

Bulldogs have big noses.
They have very short legs.

Great Danes are very tall.
They have long legs.

Dogs come in many colors.

Dalmatians have black spots.

Boxers are great dogs.
Some have brown
and white fur.

Most dogs love
a good tummy rub!

Happy dogs
move their tails.
This is called wagging!

Words to Know

boxer

bulldog

Index